66 DRUM SOLOS FOR THE MODERN DRUMMER

ROCK FUNK BLUES FUSION JAZZ

BY TOM HAPKE

Also available: *Drumming the Easy Way*, by Tom Hapke (02500191)

For more information about Tom Hapke and his books,
visit the web site *www.drums.de*

ISBN 978-1-57560-418-3

Visit our website at www.cherrylane.com

INTRODUCTION

This book presents drum solos in an easy to read form, encourages improvisation and independence, and leads to a higher level of technical achievement. It covers many aspects of modern drum playing and at the same time increases an understanding of musical notation. It contains hundreds of different grooves and fills, which can be practiced individually. To make the best use of this book, choose the solos you like most and work carefully through them from bar to bar until you can play them accurately and without stopping. Good luck and keep on drumming.

— Tom Hapke

CONTENTS

DRUM NOTATION LEGEND

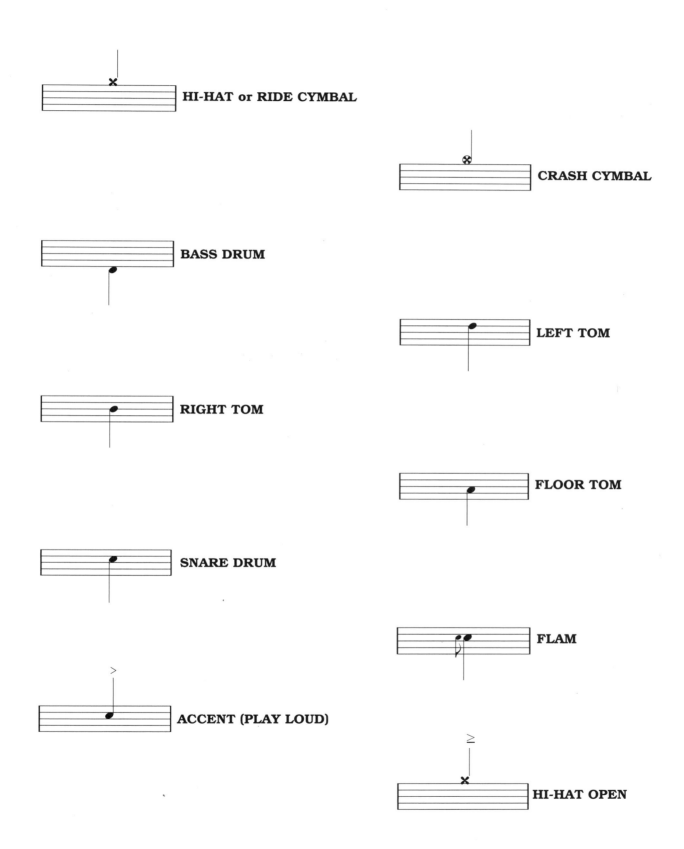

NOTE VALUES

RESTS

WHOLE NOTE

HALF NOTES

QUARTER NOTES

EIGHTH NOTES

EIGHTH NOTE TRIPLETS

SIXTEENTH NOTES

SIXTEENTH-NOTE TRIPLETS

THIRTY-SECOND NOTES

SOLO 1

Pop Rock

SOLO 2

Pop Rock

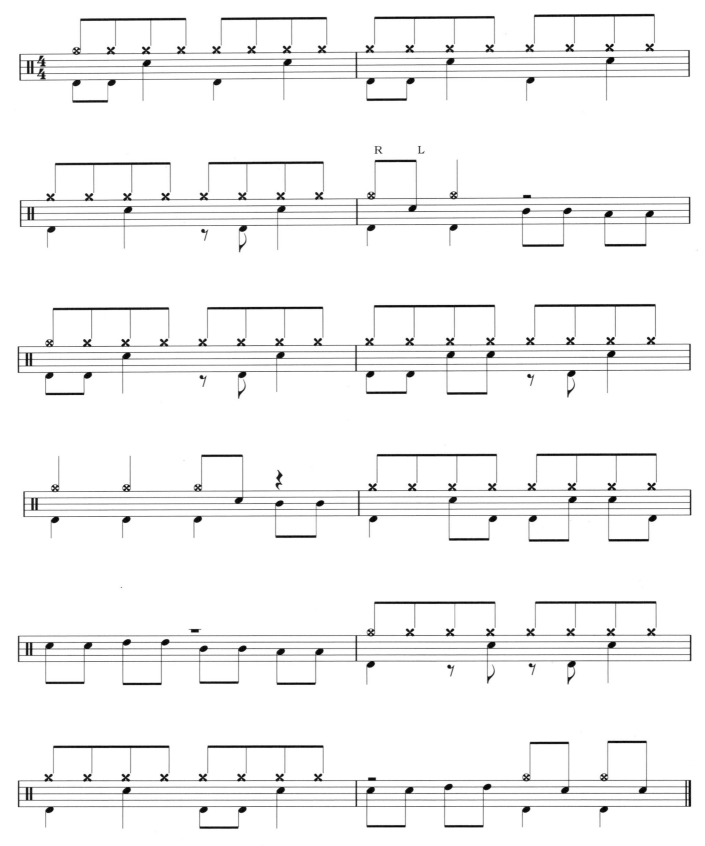

SOLO 3

Pop Rock

SOLO 4

Pop Rock

SOLO 5
Pop Rock

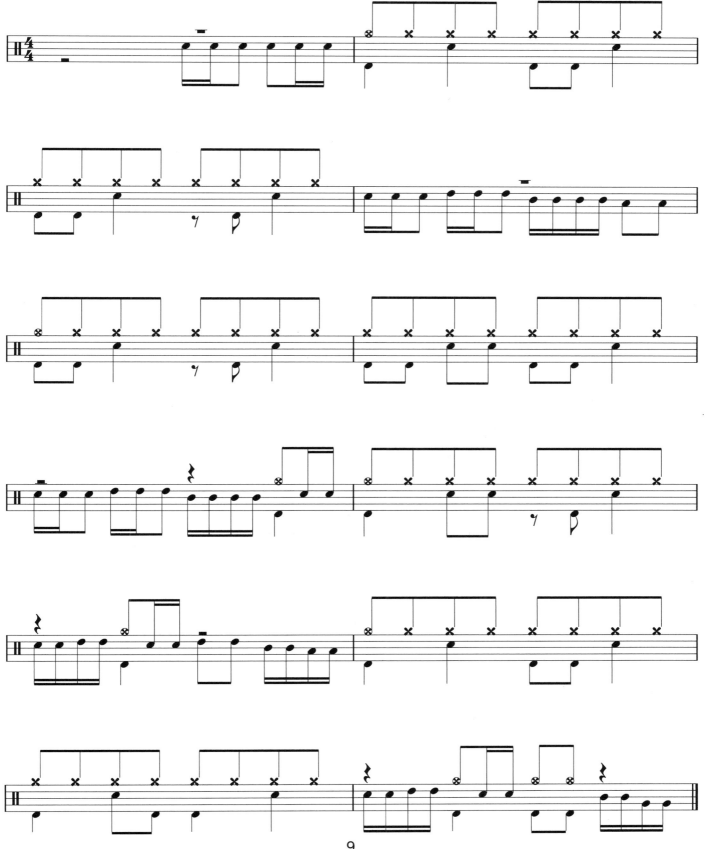

SOLO 6

Pop Rock

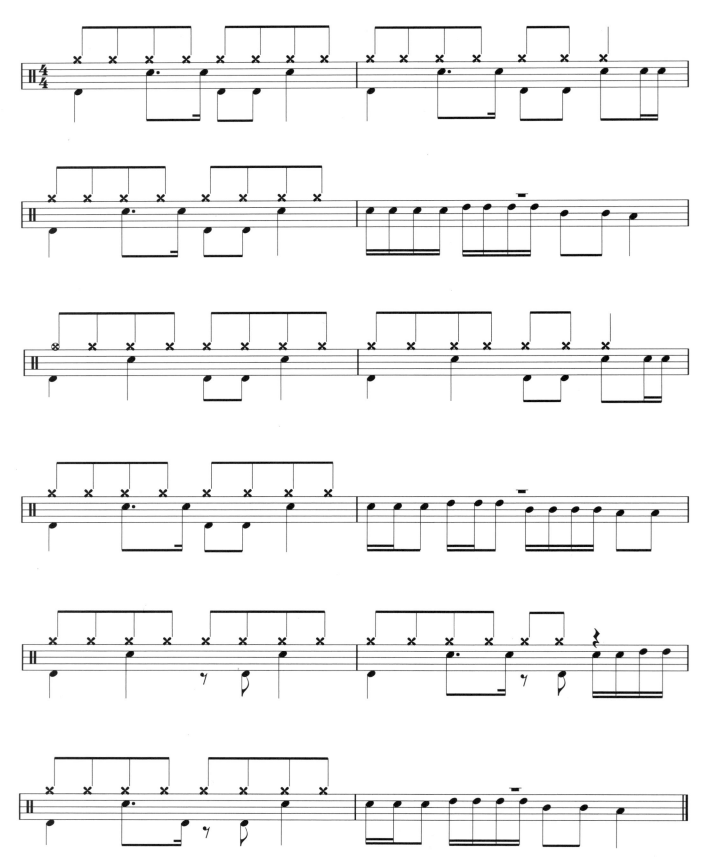

SOLO 7

Pop Rock

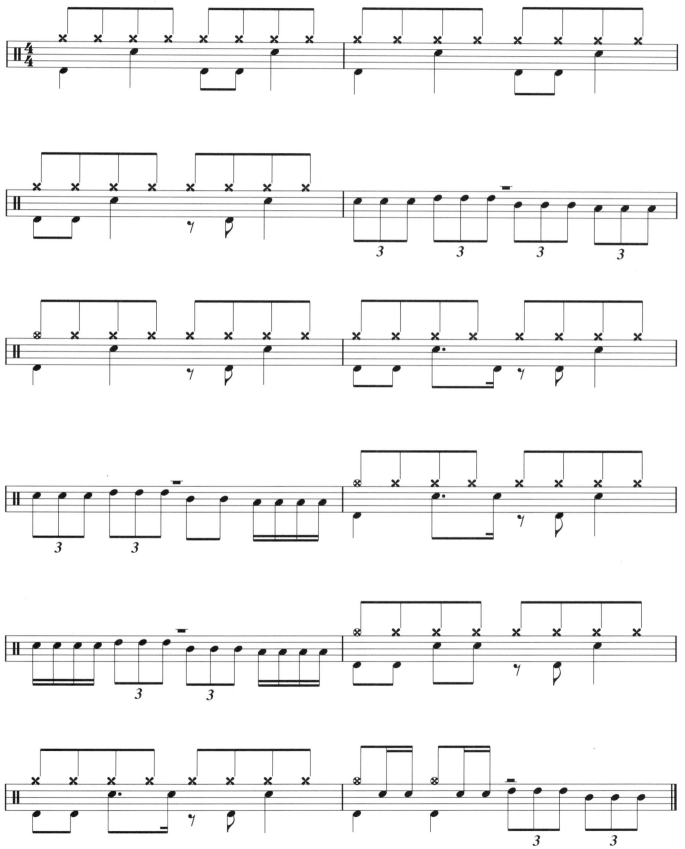

SOLO 8

Pop Rock

SOLO 9
Warm-up Solo

13

SOLO 10

Warm-up Solo

TRACK 11

SOLO 11

Warm-up Solo

TRACK 12

SOLO 12

Warm-up Solo

SOLO 13

Warm-up Solo

SOLO 14

Warm-up Solo

SOLO 15

Funk Rock

SOLO 16

Funk Rock

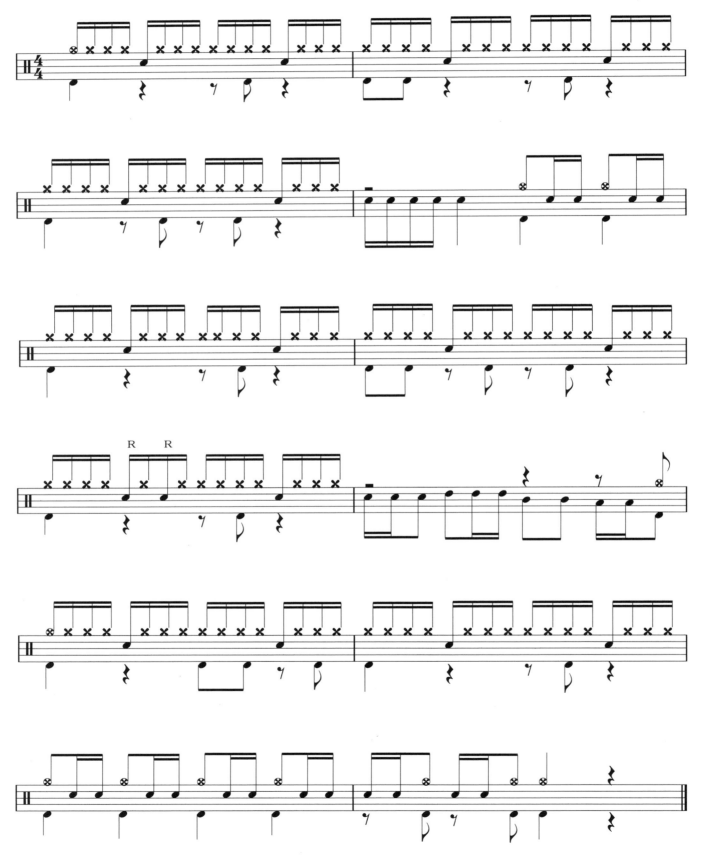

SOLO 17

Funk Rock

21

SOLO 18

Funk Rock

SOLO 19

Funk Rock

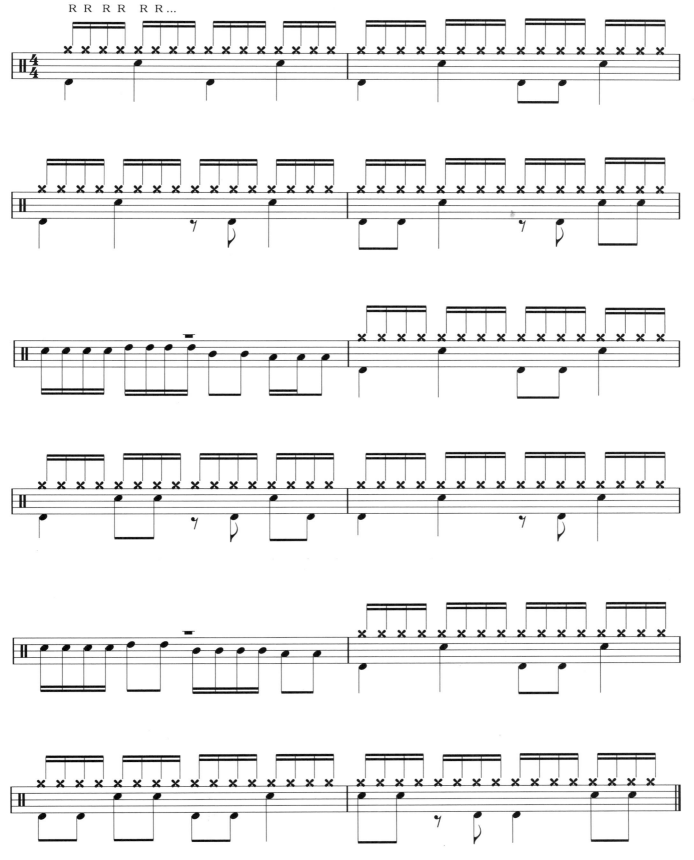

SOLO 20

Funk Rock

SOLO 21

Funk Rock

SOLO 22

Funk Rock

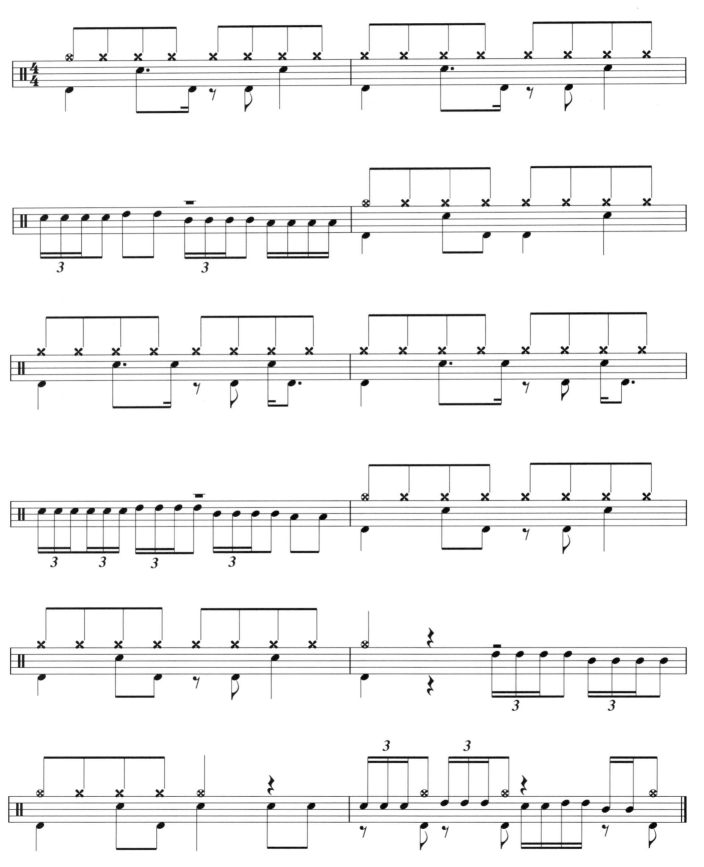

SOLO 23

Funk Rock

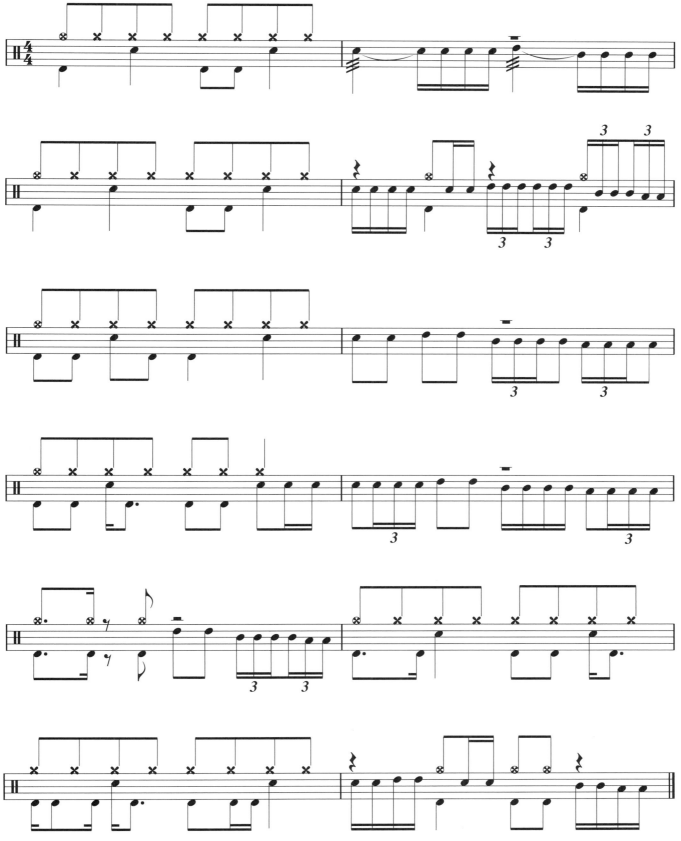

SOLO 24

Funk Rock

SOLO 25

Funk Rock

SOLO 26

Funk Rock

SOLO 27

6/8

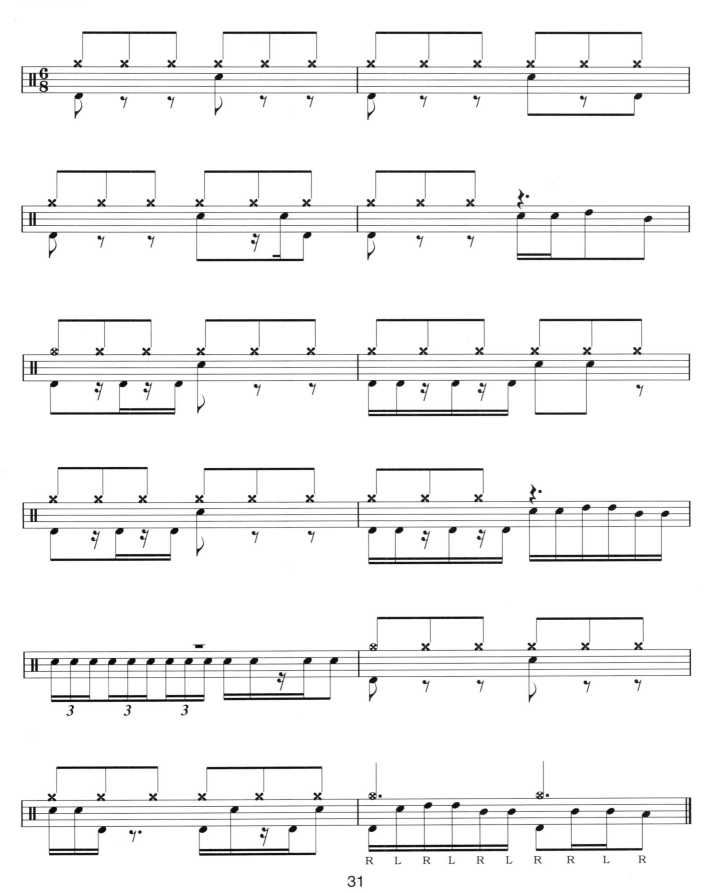

SOLO 28

6/8

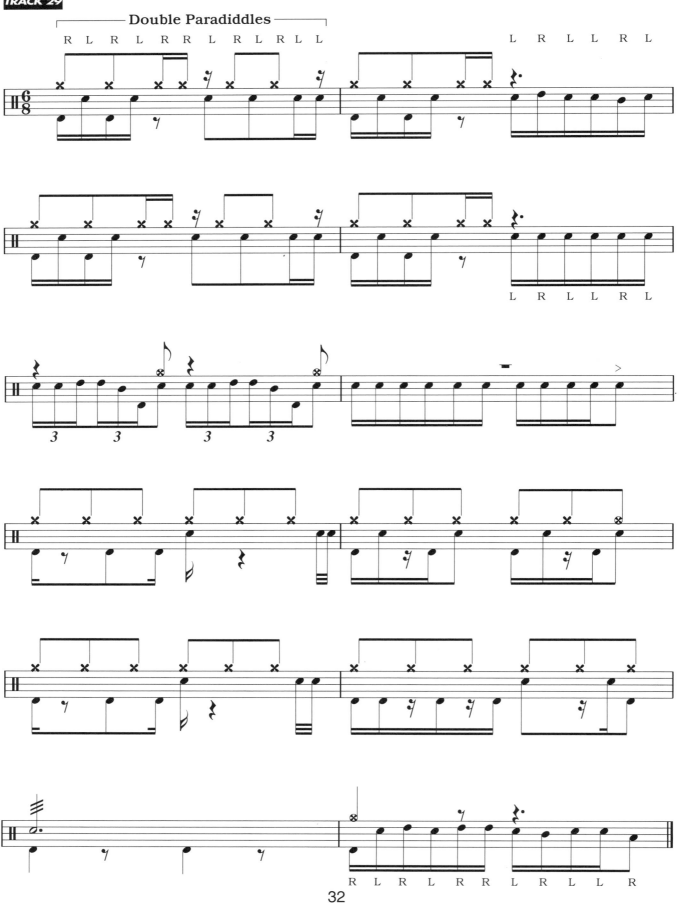

SOLO 29

7/8

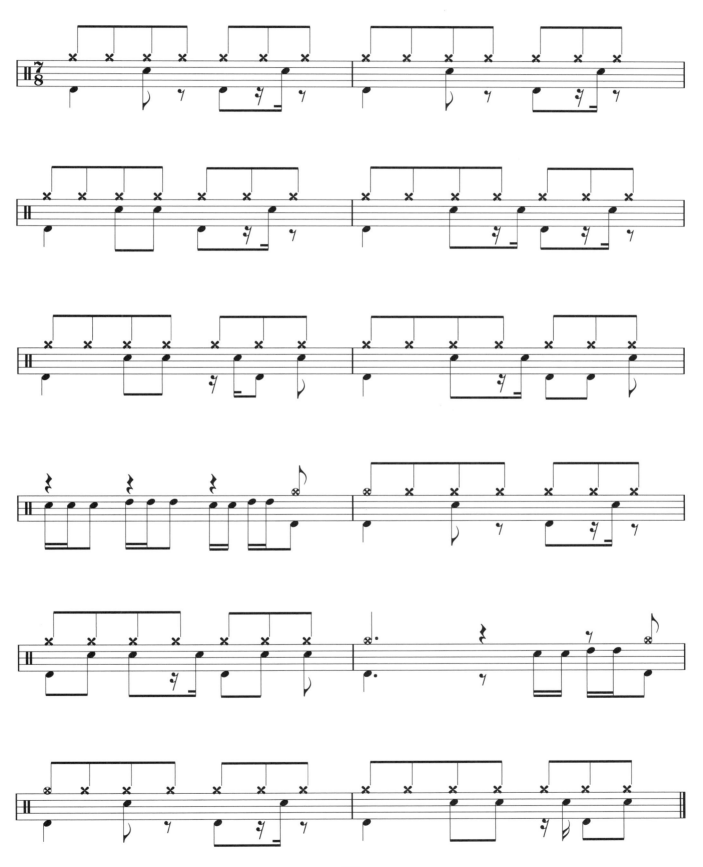

SOLO 30

7/8

TRACK 31

SOLO 31

Rock Fusion

SOLO 32

Rock Fusion

SOLO 33

Rock Fusion

SOLO 34

Rock Fusion

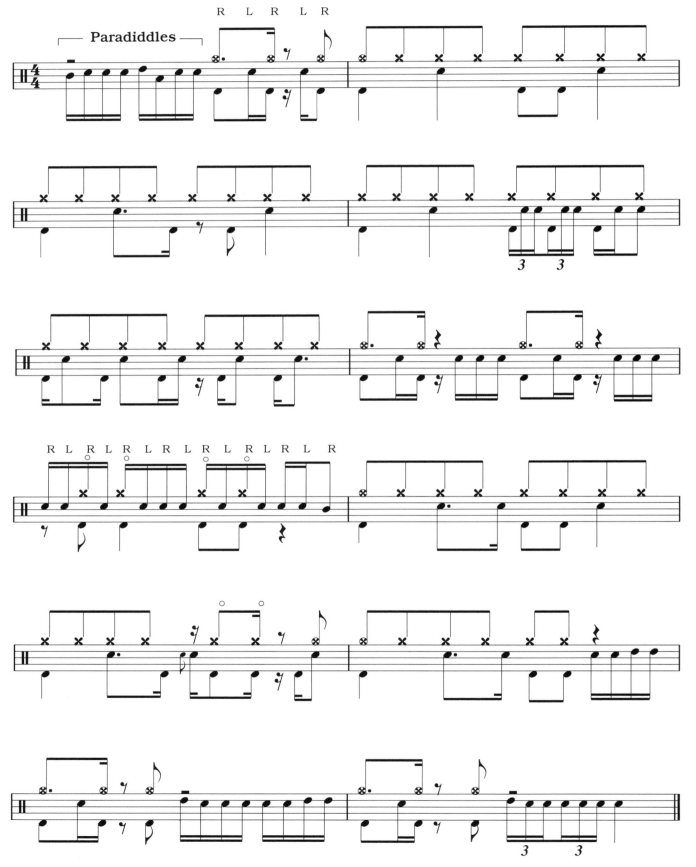

SOLO 35

Rock Fusion

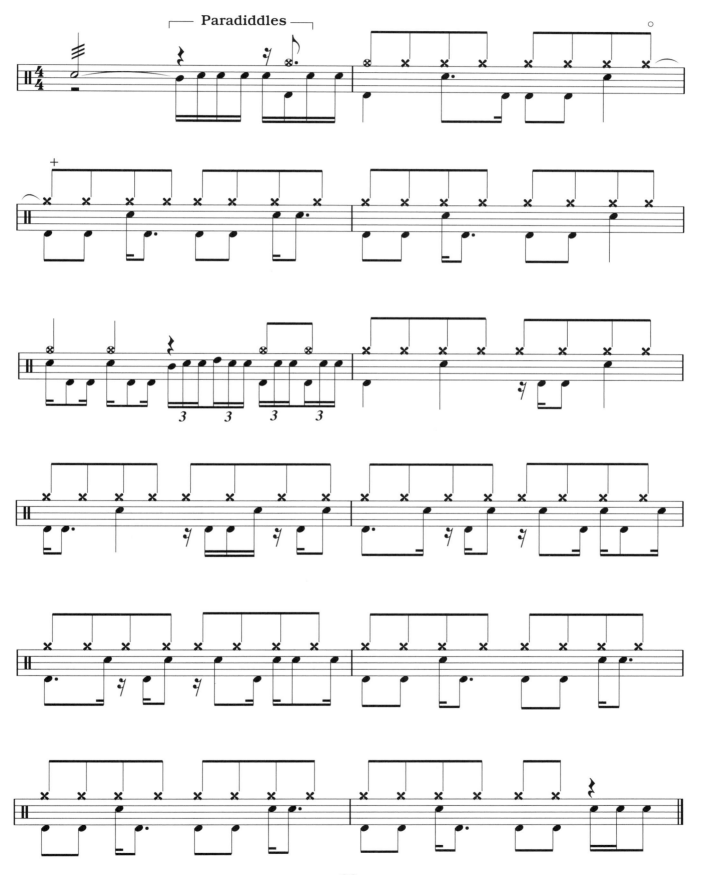

SOLO 36

Rock Fusion

SOLO 37

Rock Fusion

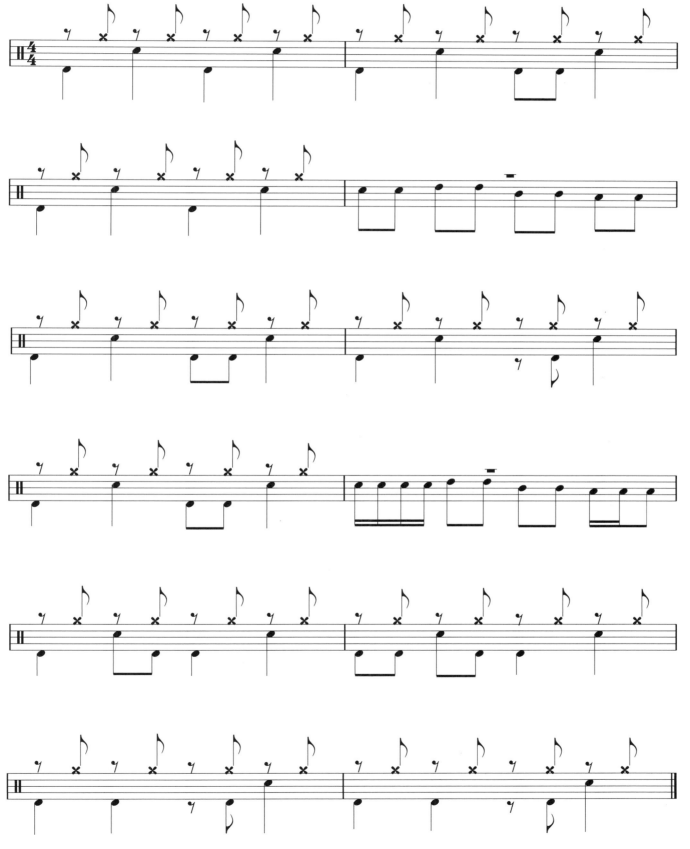

SOLO 38

Rock Fusion

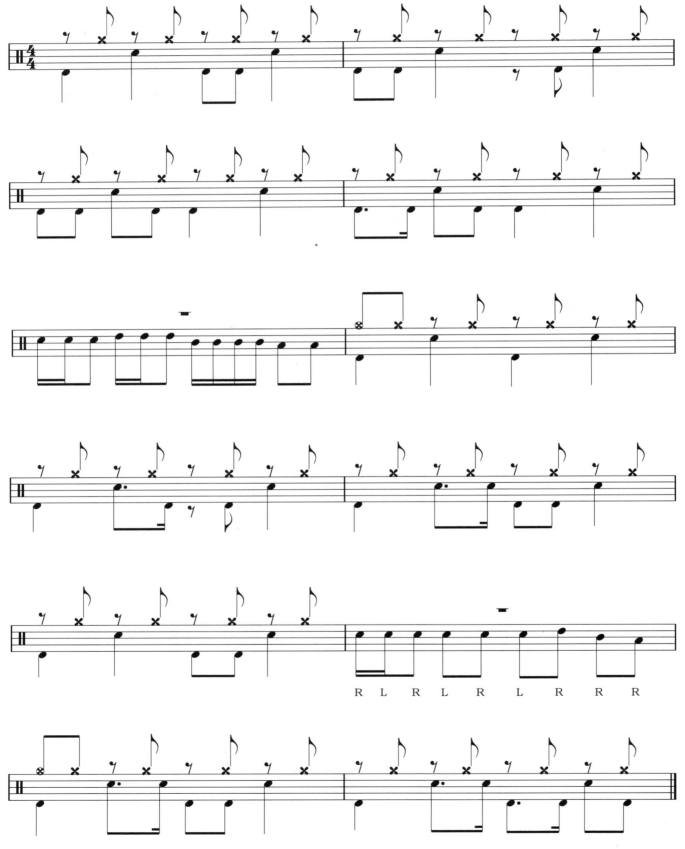

SOLO 39

Rock Fusion

SOLO 40

Rock Fusion

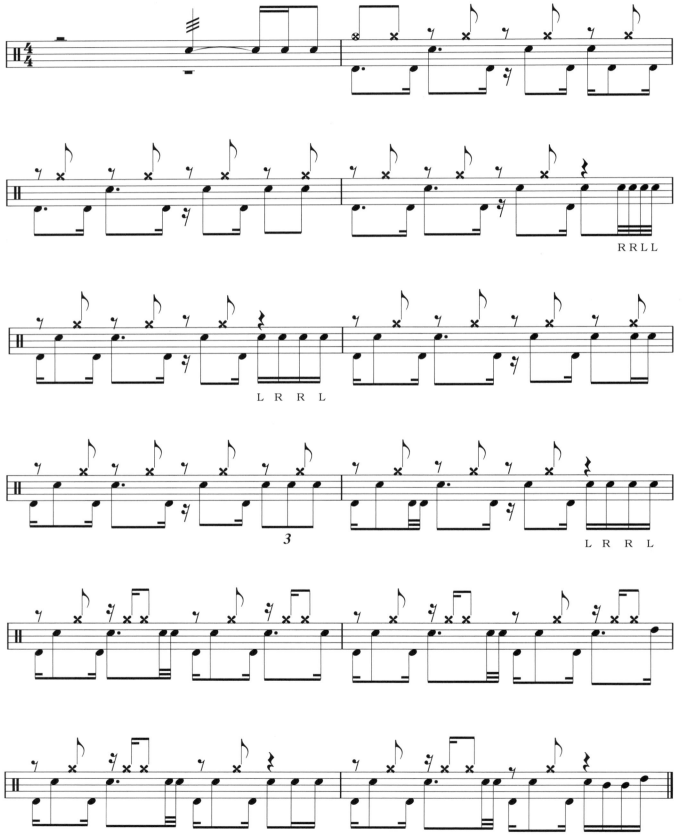

SOLO 41

Rock Fusion

SOLO 42

Rock Fusion

SOLO 43

Hard Rock

SOLO 44

Hard Rock

SOLO 45

Hard Rock

SOLO 46

Hard Rock

SOLO 47

Jazz

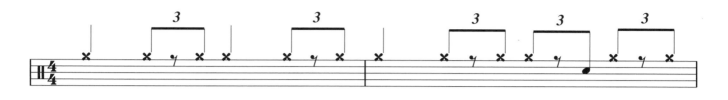

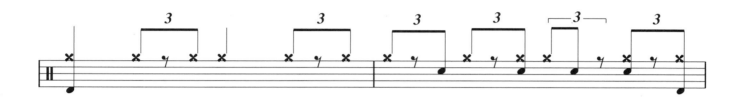

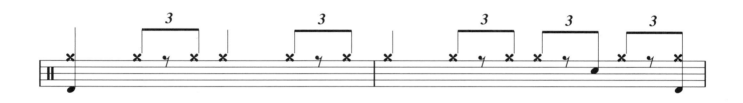

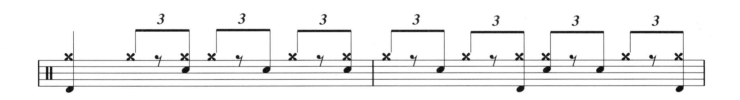

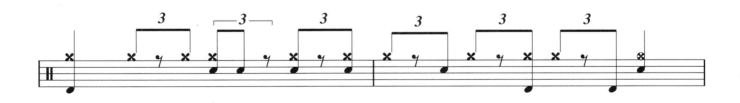

SOLO 48

Jazz

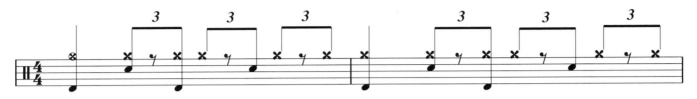

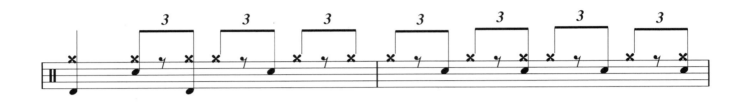

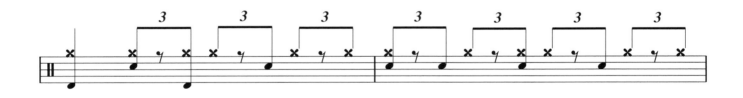

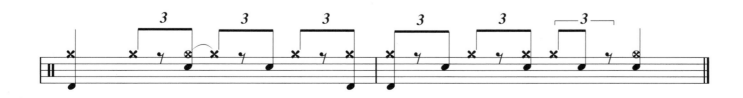

SOLO 49

Jazz

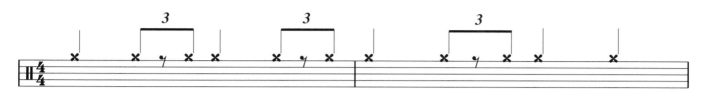

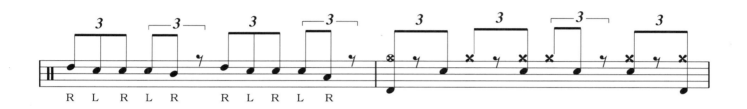

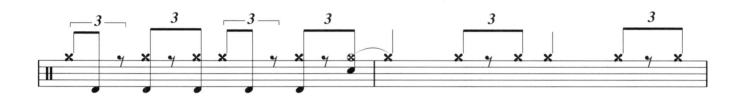

SOLO 50

Jazz

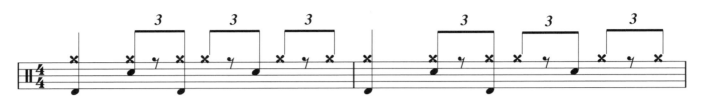
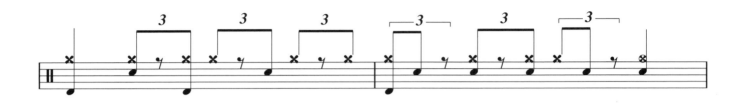
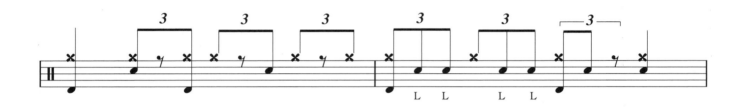
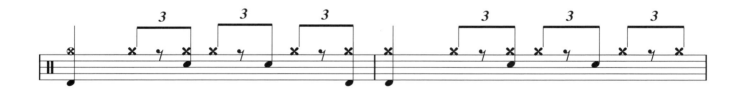
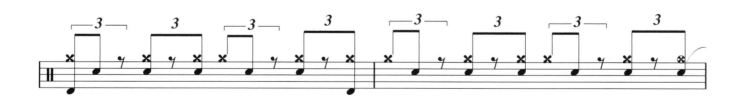
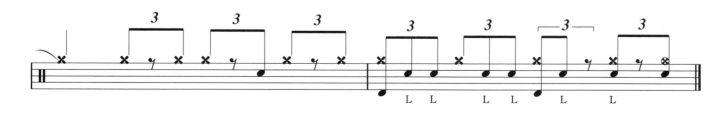

SOLO 51

Jazz

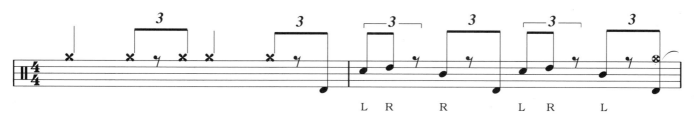

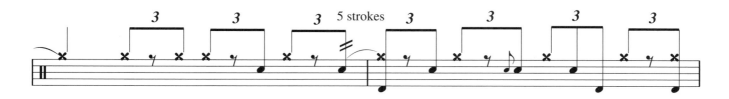

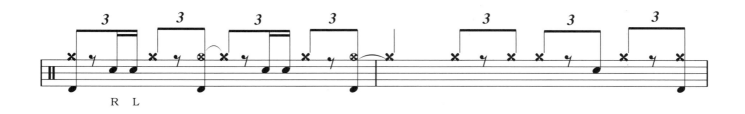

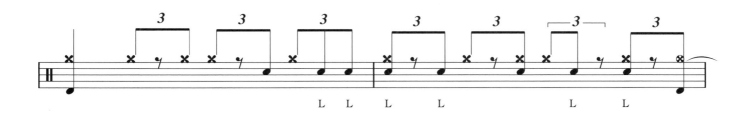

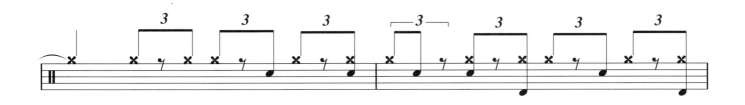

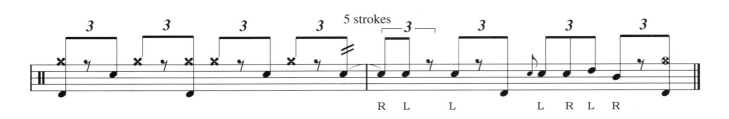

SOLO 52

Shuffle

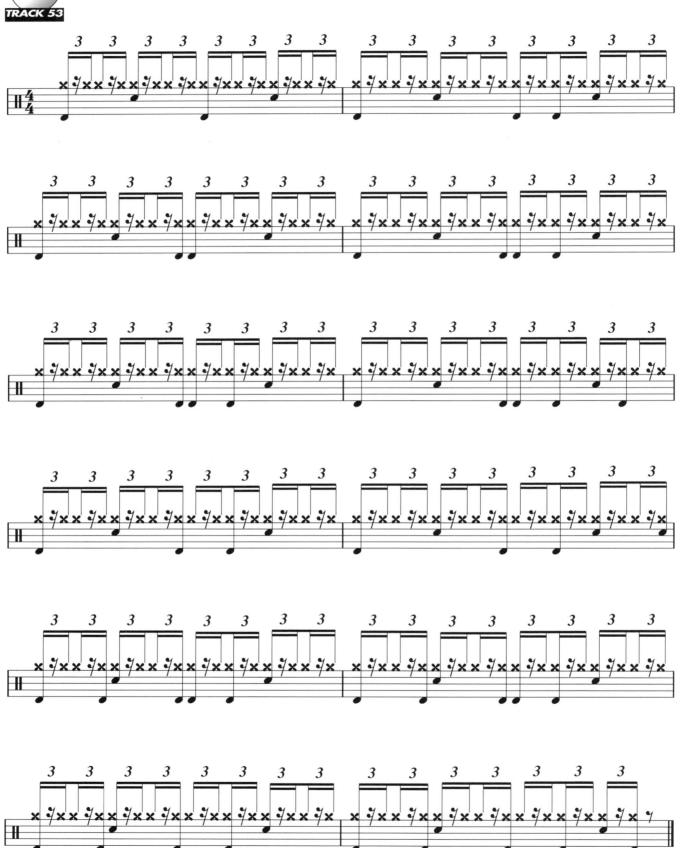

SOLO 53

Shuffle

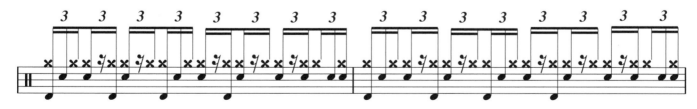

SOLO 54

Shuffle

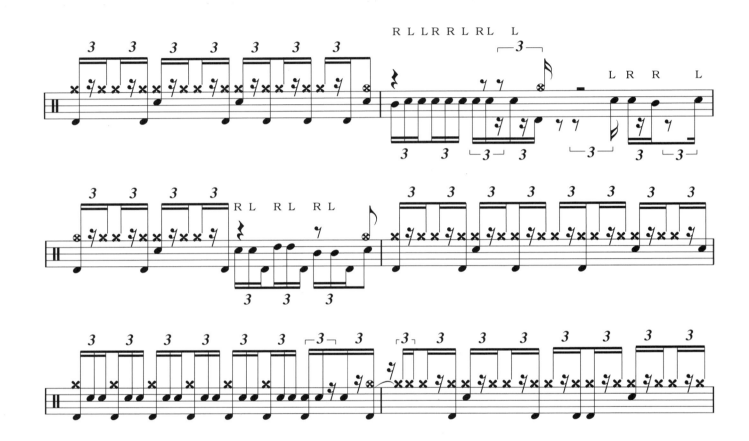

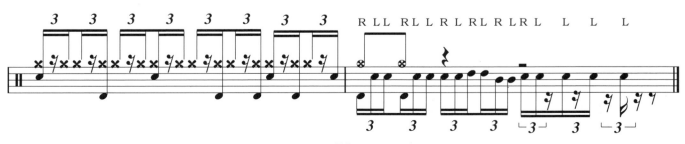

SOLO 55

Jazz Fusion

SOLO 56

Jazz Fusion

SOLO 57

Jazz Fusion

SOLO 58

Jazz Fusion

SOLO 59

Jazz Fusion

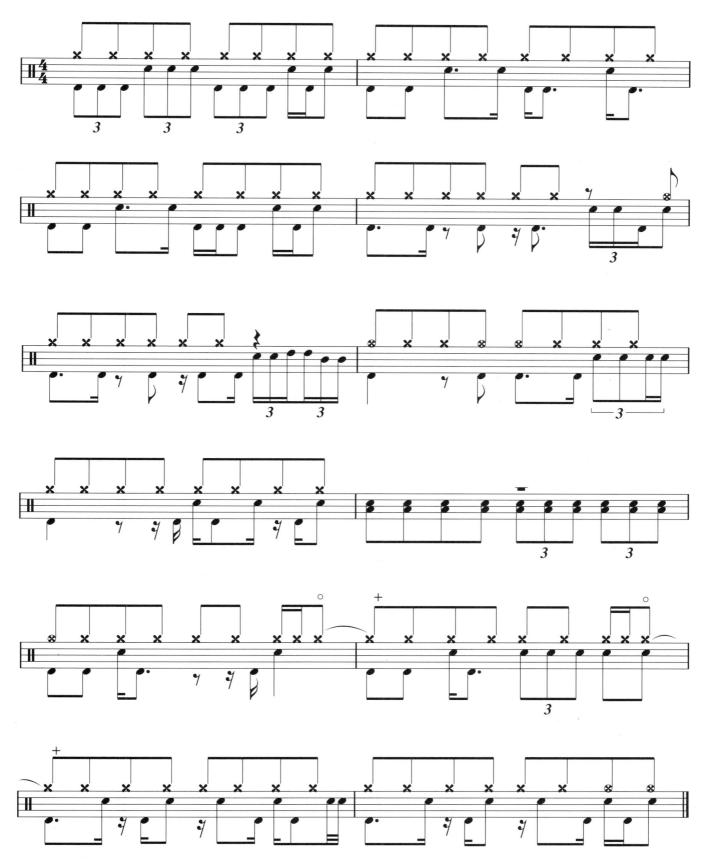

SOLO 60

Jazz Fusion

SOLO 61

Jazz Fusion

SOLO 62

Jazz Fusion

SOLO 63

Jazz Fusion

SOLO 64

Jazz Fusion

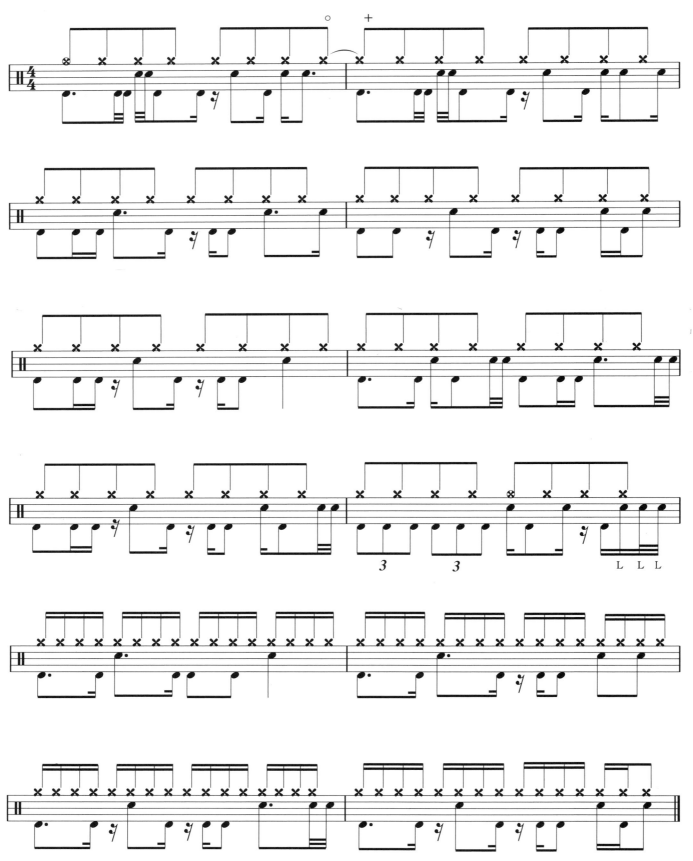

SOLO 65

Jazz Fusion

SOLO 66

Jazz Fusion

MORE HOT DRUM BOOKS AND DVDs FROM CHERRY LANE

STEVEN ADLER'S GETTING STARTED WITH ROCK DRUMMING DVD VIDEO
Taught by the Legendary Former Guns N' Roses Drummer!
02501387 DVD.......................$29.99

AFRO-CARIBBEAN DRUM GROOVES
by Chuck Silverman
02500370 Book/CD Pack.......................$14.95

THE BOOK OF FUNK BEATS
Grooves for Snare, Bass, and Hi-hat
by David Lewitt
02500953 Book/CD Pack.......................$14.99

PONCHO SANCHEZ' CONGA COOKBOOK
by Poncho Sanchez with Chuck Silverman
02500278 Book/CD Pack.......................$16.95

DRUM EXERCISES FOR THE POP, FUNK, AND R&B PLAYER
by Ralph Johnson
02500827 Book/CD Pack.......................$14.99

DRUMMING THE EASY WAY!
The Beginner's Guide to Playing Drums for Students and Teachers
by Tom Hapke
02500876 Book/CD Pack.......................$19.95
02500191 Book Only.......................$12.95

DRUMMING THE EASY WAY! VOLUME 2
by Tom Hapke
02501060 Book/CD Pack.......................$17.95
02501064 Book Only.......................$12.95

LATIN FUNK CONNECTION DVD VIDEO
taught by Chuck Silverman
02501417 DVD.......................$24.99

BEST OF THE DAVE MATTHEWS BAND FOR DRUMS
02500184 Play-It-Like-It-Is Drum.......................$19.95

DAVE MATTHEWS BAND – FAN FAVORITES FOR DRUMS
02500643 Play-It-Like-It-Is Drum.......................$19.95

METALLICA – ...AND JUSTICE FOR ALL
02503504 Play-It-Like-It-Is Drum.......................$18.95

METALLICA – BLACK
02503509 Play-It-Like-It-Is Drum.......................$18.95

METALLICA: CLASSIC SONGS – DRUM LEGENDARY LICKS DVD VIDEO
taught by Jack E. Roth
A Step-By-Step Breakdown of Metallica's Drum Grooves and Fills
02500839 DVD.......................$24.95

METALLICA – DEATH MAGNETIC
02501315 Play-It-Like-It-Is Drum.......................$19.99

METALLICA – DRUM LEGENDARY LICKS
taught by Gregory Beyer
02500172 Book/CD Pack.......................$19.95

METALLICA – DRUM LEGENDARY LICKS 1983-1988 DVD VIDEO
A Step-by-Step Breakdown of Metallica's Drum Grooves and Fills
featuring Nathan Kilen
02500482 DVD.......................$24.95

METALLICA – DRUM LEGENDARY LICKS 1988-1997 DVD VIDEO
A Step-by-Step Breakdown of Metallica's Drum Grooves and Fills
featuring Nathan Kilen
02500485 DVD.......................$24.95

METALLICA – GARAGE INC.
02500077 Play-It-Like-It-Is Drum.......................$18.95

METALLICA – KILL 'EM ALL
02503508 Play-It-Like-It-Is Drum.......................$18.95

LEARN TO PLAY DRUMS WITH METALLICA
by Greg Beyer
02500190 Book/CD Pack.......................$14.95

LEARN TO PLAY DRUMS WITH METALLICA – VOLUME 2
by Dan Gross
02500887 Book/CD Pack.......................$15.95

METALLICA – MASTER OF PUPPETS
02503502 Play-It-Like-It-Is Drum.......................$18.95

METALLICA – RE-LOAD
02503517 Play-It-Like-It-Is Drum.......................$18.95

METALLICA – RIDE THE LIGHTNING
02503507 Play-It-Like-It-Is Drum.......................$17.95

METALLICA – ST. ANGER
02500640 Play-It-Like-It-Is Drum.......................$19.95

METALLICA'S LARS ULRICH
02506306 Book/CD Pack.......................$17.95

PONCHO SANCHEZ DVD VIDEO
Fundamentals of Latin Music for the Rhythm Section
featuring the Poncho Sanchez Latin Jazz Band
02500729 DVD.......................$24.95

1001 DRUM GROOVES
The Complete Resource for Every Drummer
by Steve Mansfield
02500337 Book.......................$12.95

66 DRUM SOLOS FOR THE MODERN DRUMMER
by Tom Hapke
02500319 Book/CD Pack.......................$16.95

RUSH – LEGENDARY LICKS FOR DRUMS DVD VIDEO
Taught and Performed by Jamie Borden
02500628 DVD.......................$24.95

See your local music retailer or contact:

cherry lane music company

EXCLUSIVELY DISTRIBUTED BY
HAL•LEONARD® CORPORATION
7777 W. BLUEMOUND RD. P.O. BOX 13819 MILWAUKEE, WI 53213

Prices, contents, and availability subject to change without notice.

0909

MORE GREAT PUBLICATIONS FROM
TOM HAPKE AND CHERRY LANE MUSIC

66 DRUM SOLOS FOR THE MODERN DRUMMER

ROCK • FUNK • BLUES • FUSION • JAZZ

by Tom Hapke

66 Drum Solos for the Modern Drummer presents drum solos in all styles of music in an easy-to-read format. These solos are designed to help improve your technique, independence, improvisational skills, and reading ability on the drums and at the same time provide you with some cool licks that you can use right away in your own playing.

"66 Drum Solos for the Modern Drummer has great information and would be a challenge to any drummer."

– Joe Porcaro

02500319 Book/CD Pack $16.95
02501624 Book/DVD Pack $19.99

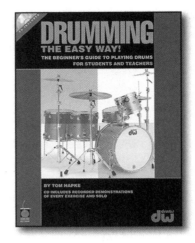

DRUMMING THE EASY WAY!

THE BEGINNER'S GUIDE TO PLAYING DRUMS FOR STUDENTS AND TEACHERS

by Tom Hapke

This bestseller takes the beginning drummer through the paces – from reading simple exercises to playing great grooves and fills. Each lesson includes a preparatory exercise and a solo. Concepts and rhythms are introduced one at a time, so growth is natural and easy. Features large, clear musical print, intensive treatment of each individual drum figure, solos following each exercise to motivate students, and more!

"I highly recommend (this book) to students and teachers. The information is easy to understand and progresses at a good pace."

– Joe Porcaro

02500191 Book Only $12.95
02500876 Book/CD Pack $19.95

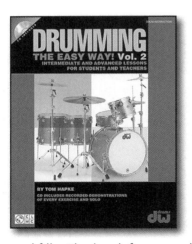

DRUMMING THE EASY WAY! VOLUME 2

INTERMEDIATE AND ADVANCED LESSONS FOR STUDENTS AND TEACHERS

by Tom Hapke

This second volume takes the intermediate drummer through the paces – from reading exercises to playing great grooves and fills. The book features clear and large musical print, intensive treatment of each individual drum figure, and drum solos following each exercise to motivate and increase the "fun factor" for students.

02501064 Book Only $12.95
02501060 Book/CD Pack $17.95

STUDIO ESSENTIALS

by Tom Hapke

Whether you're a beginner looking for clear instructions on the fundamental techniques of recording, or you're a seasoned pro in search of a reference guide of key concepts, *Studio Essentials* is for you. With instructions on dozens of techniques and concepts written in a "just the facts" manner, you'll be up and running in no time. Over 100 helpful photos and diagrams help to show the way. Topics include room acoustics, microphones, effects, exciters, enhancers, equalizers, filters, and tips and tricks. This is an excellent resource and reference guide for home hobbyists and experienced professionals, with valuable information on miking techniques.

02501134 Reference Book $17.99

See your local music dealer or contact:

EXCLUSIVELY DISTRIBUTED BY
HAL•LEONARD® CORPORATION

7777 W. BLUEMOUND RD. P.O. BOX 13819 MILWAUKEE, WI 53213

Prices, contents, and availability subject to change without notice.